Face to face, he is relaxed, simple, and charming—
he seems incapable of wrongdoing or
of sanctioning any crime. But this is no more than
a facade. He is at heart a manipulator—charm
and generosity are his two greatest weapons.
He will say anything to win the affection of
the person he is with—but thinks nothing of saying
exactly the opposite to his next visitor.
He kills rationally and coolly.

Godfrey Lule, former Ugandan
minister of justice, 1977

For my father, who said he loved history
"because it brings the dead back to life."

Photographs © 2010: AP Images: 67 bottom (camerapix), 98 (Bill Kostroun), 47 (Time Life Inc.), 11, 13, 59, 64 top, 65 bottom, 66 top, 67 center, 78, 97, 105, 112; Corbis Images/Bettmann: 63 bottom, 67 top, 72, 114, 116, 118; Getty Images: 65 top, 88 (AFP), 24 (James Burke), 53 (Central Press), 42 (Terry Fincher & Ron Case), 61 (Keystone), 109 (Keystone/Hulton Archive), 63 top (Albert McCabe), 28, 29 (Popperfoto), 62 bottom (George Rodger), 104, 110 (Rolls Press/Popperfoto), 18 (Terrence Spencer); Magnum Photos: 66 center (Abbas), 64 center, 93 (David Hurn), 62 top (George Rodger), 66 bottom (Alex Webb); NEWSCOM: 64 bottom; Northwestern University, Chicago, IL: 20 (Winterton Collection of East African Photographs/Melville J. Herskovits Library of African Studies/Object 56-1-21-1); Photoshot/WpN: 65 center, 83; The Image Works: 21 (Mary Evans Picture Library), 43, 63 center (TopFoto), 40 (Topham).

Illustrations by XNR Productions, Inc.: 4, 5, 8, 9, 45
Cover art, page 8 inset by Mark Summers
Chapter art by Raphael Montoliu

Library of Congress Cataloging-in-Publication Data
Dougherty, Steve, 1948–
Idi Amin / Steve Dougherty.
p. cm. — (A wicked history)
Includes bibliographical references and index.
ISBN-13: 978-0-531-20754-3 (lib. bdg.) 978-0-531-22354-3 (pbk.)
ISBN-10: 0-531-20754-4 (lib. bdg.) 0-531-22354-X (pbk.)
1. Amin, Idi, 1925–2003–Juvenile literature. 2.
Presidents–Uganda–Biography–Juvenile literature. 3.
Uganda–History–1971–1979–Juvenile literature. I. Title.
DT433.28.A45D68 2010
967.6104'2092–dc22
[B]

2009034158

Tod Olson, Series Editor
Marie O'Neill, Art Director
Allicette Torres, Cover Design
SimonSays Design! Book Design and Production
Content consultant: Michelle R. Moyd, Assistant professor,
Department of History, Indiana University

© 2010 Scholastic Inc.

All rights reserved. Published by Franklin Watts, an imprint of Scholastic Inc.
Published simultaneously in Canada. Printed in the United States of America.

SCHOLASTIC, FRANKLIN WATTS, A WICKED HISTORY, and associated logos
are trademarks and/or registered trademarks of Scholastic Inc.

1 2 3 4 5 6 7 8 9 10 R 19 18 17 16 15 14 13 12 11 10   23

A WiCKED HISTORY™
20TH CENTURY

Idi Amin

STEVE DOUGHERTY

Franklin Watts®
An Imprint of Scholastic Inc.
New York   Toronto   London   Auckland   Sydney
Mexico City   New Delhi   Hong Kong
Danbury, Connecticut

The World of
IDI AMIN

In 1971, Idi Amin seized control of the fertile nation of Uganda—known as the "Pearl of Africa"—and plunged it into poverty and violence.

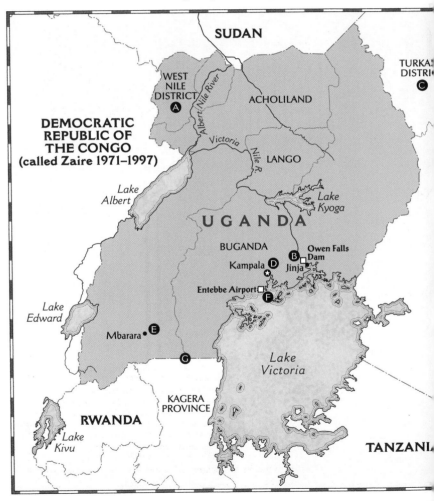

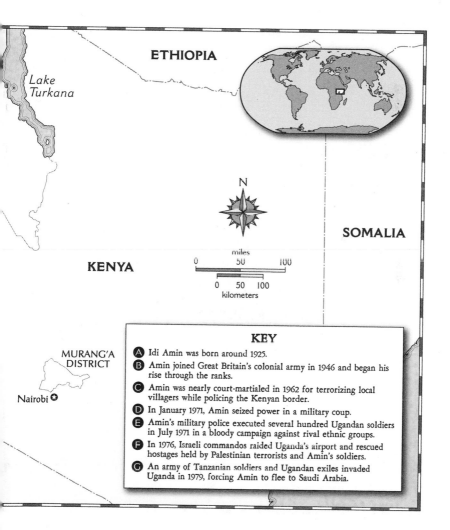

ETHIOPIA

Lake Turkana

SOMALIA

KENYA

N

miles
0   50   100

0   50   100
kilometers

MURANG'A
DISTRICT

Nairobi ⊘

KEY

Ⓐ Idi Amin was born around 1925.

Ⓑ Amin joined Great Britain's colonial army in 1946 and began his rise through the ranks.

Ⓒ Amin was nearly court-martialed in 1962 for terrorizing local villagers while policing the Kenyan border.

Ⓓ In January 1971, Amin seized power in a military coup.

Ⓔ Amin's military police executed several hundred Ugandan soldiers in July 1971 in a bloody campaign against rival ethnic groups.

Ⓕ In 1976, Israeli commandos raided Uganda's airport and rescued hostages held by Palestinian terrorists and Amin's soldiers.

Ⓖ An army of Tanzanian soldiers and Ugandan exiles invaded Uganda in 1979, forcing Amin to flee to Saudi Arabia.

TABLE OF CONTENTS

PART 3: REIGN OF TERROR

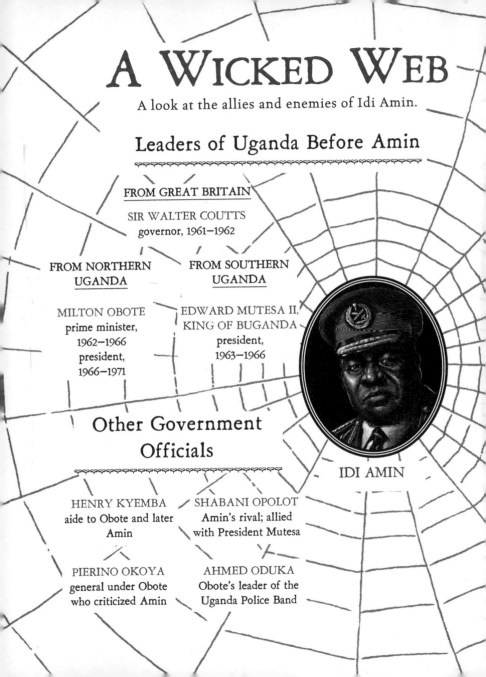

A WICKED WEB

A look at the allies and enemies of Idi Amin.

Leaders of Uganda Before Amin

FROM GREAT BRITAIN

SIR WALTER COUTTS
governor, 1961–1962

FROM NORTHERN UGANDA

MILTON OBOTE
prime minister,
1962–1966
president,
1966–1971

FROM SOUTHERN UGANDA

EDWARD MUTESA II,
KING OF BUGANDA
president,
1963–1966

Other Government Officials

HENRY KYEMBA
aide to Obote and later
Amin

SHABANI OPOLOT
Amin's rival; allied
with President Mutesa

PIERINO OKOYA
general under Obote
who criticized Amin

AHMED ODUKA
Obote's leader of the
Uganda Police Band

IDI AMIN

Critics and Victims

NICK STROH
American journalist

ROBERT SIEDLE
American professor and friend
of Stroh's

DAVID JEFFREYS JONES
British judge who
investigated Amin

YASMIN ALIBHAI-BROWN
Ugandan-born Asian
exiled by Amin

BENEDICTO KIWANUKA
chief justice of
Uganda's supreme court

DAVID MARTIN
British journalist

DORA BLOCH
airline passenger taken hostage
and killed

JANANI LUWUN
archbishop of Anglican Church
of Uganda

World Leaders

MUAMMAR GADDAFI
dictator of Libya

JULIUS NYERERE
president of Tanzania

YOWERI MUSEVENI
became president of Uganda
in 1986

On A DAY OF SUCH BRIGHT PROMISE, the horrifying scene seemed out of place.

It was January 31, 1971, Henry Kyemba's first day at work in the offices of Uganda's popular new president. It felt like a new beginning—both for himself and for his country.

Kyemba's boss, President Idi Amin, was already a hero in Uganda. The people knew him as a dashing soldier and a famous athlete. While rising through the ranks of the army, Amin had won Uganda's light heavyweight boxing championship and held it for nine years. He stood well over six feet tall and weighed nearly 250 pounds. In the ring and on the battlefield, he had a reputation for battering opponents into submission. But in person, he was usually good-humored and charming. Newspapers had already begun to call him "Big Daddy."

TWO DAYS AFTER SEIZING POWER
in a military coup, Amin (far right) holds his first
press conference as the president of Uganda.

Just a week earlier, Amin had ousted the previous
president, the corrupt Milton Obote, in a military coup.
Almost all Ugandans applauded the change. Here, they
thought, was a leader who would bring freedom and
democracy to Uganda.

Amin quickly gave his admirers plenty of reason for
optimism. He promised to hold free elections. He shut

down Obote's secret police squads and freed political prisoners. He appointed talented and experienced ministers to his new cabinet. He even allowed officials from Obote's government to keep their jobs.

But on Kyemba's first day at work, as he gazed out his office window, he was shocked to see a group of soldiers chasing a man down the street. The man was someone Kyemba knew—a high-ranking military adviser from the Obote administration.

Kyemba's shock turned to horror when he saw the soldiers chase the military adviser into a nearby house. After a burst of gunfire, the soldiers came back out, dragging the bullet-riddled body of the adviser with them.

Disturbing as the incident was, Kyemba told himself that the adviser must have been involved in some terrible crime, perhaps even a plot to assassinate the new president.

Only much later would Kyemba realize what he had witnessed. The killing that day on the streets of

TWO DAYS AFTER AMIN'S COUP, one of his soldiers clubs
a prisoner with his rifle. Amin had promised to bring peace
to Uganda, but his soldiers were murdering officials who had
worked for the previous president.

Kampala was no isolated act of violence. It was the
beginning of a bloody reign of terror launched by
Idi Amin, the man who claimed to be the savior of
Uganda. Before the terror was over, it would claim
hundreds of thousands of lives and tear an entire
nation apart.

PART 1

TRAINING OF A TYRANT

CHAPTER 1

Coming of Age

Idi Amin becomes a
WARRIOR WITHOUT AN ARMY.

IDI AMIN BEGAN HIS LIFE A LONG WAY from a presidential office. He was born in a mud hut in the West Nile district, a remote region in northern Uganda near the border of Sudan. The year was probably 1925, though no one kept official records. There were no hospitals, doctors, or nurses for miles around.

Amin's mother was undernourished and frail. She struggled for hours to give birth, screaming through the night. Village midwives who attended her feared for her life.

Finally, before dawn, the cry of her baby boy was heard. And as soon as villagers saw the baby, they understood why his mother had such an agonizing delivery. The boy weighed 12 pounds and was bigger than any newborn most people had seen.

Amin's early life was not much easier than his birth. His father scratched out a meager living as a farmer and goatherd. The land around his village was barren and dry. Villagers consulted shamans and placed stones on the dry ground in a ritual arrangement that was meant to bring rain. If the rain didn't come, the village suffered through drought and starvation.

When Amin was still young, his mother fled West Nile after a violent argument with her hotheaded husband. She took her son to Buganda, a rich and fertile province in southern Uganda. Amin spent a few years in school while his mother labored in the fields of a sugarcane plantation.

At the age of 13, Amin took part in a coming-of-age ritual celebrated by his father's ethnic group, the

VILLAGERS IN THE KINGDOM OF BUGANDA,
the wealthiest region in the colony of Uganda. Amin
moved to Buganda when he was a boy.

Kakwa. A Kakwa elder used a machete to make a set
of small slashes on the right side of Amin's face. The
slash wounds left Amin with three small scars—a

permanent reminder to himself and all who met him that he was a Kakwa warrior.

But by then, the bloody ceremony no longer meant what it had for his ancestors. The warriors who dominated life in Uganda were not the Kakwa. They were the officers of the British army, which decades earlier had conquered Amin's ancestors and 30 other ethnic groups in the region.

In 1894, the British had combined the homelands of these groups to create the colony of Uganda. Now the warriors from these conquered peoples no longer fought for their own people. They served under British officers in a regiment of black soldiers known as the King's African Rifles (KAR). Their job was to keep the peace between East Africa's rival ethnic groups and to put down rebellions against British rule.

For many African boys like Amin, the KAR offered the only way out of the grinding poverty and boredom of village life. So Amin was thrilled when his mother got a job cooking and cleaning for a unit of the King's

SOLDIERS IN THE KING'S AFRICAN RIFLES. This colonial
army fought for the British Empire's interests in East Africa. Amin
joined the King's African Rifles when he was a young man.

African Rifles. He moved with her into the barracks at
the British military base in Jinja.

Under the eye of Uganda's colonial rulers, Idi
Amin's training as a modern-day warrior began.

Under Colonial Rule

BRITISH EXPLORERS FIRST CAME TO THE REGION of Uganda in the 1860s. Hunters, traders, plantation owners, and miners soon followed, searching for ways to make money in Africa. With them came the British army, intent on protecting the British Empire's economic interests.

When the British arrived, the region was home to more than 30 ethnic groups, which often went to war with each other over land, cattle, and other resources. The leader of the most powerful group, the *kabaka* (king) of Buganda, saw that his weapons were no match for the modern rifles and cannons of the British army. In 1890, the kabaka agreed to a treaty that gave the British the right to govern his kingdom.

The British gradually united the remaining ethnic groups into the colony they called Uganda. But inter-ethnic hostilities smoldered under British rule. Years later, under a dictator named Idi Amin, they would help fuel a firestorm of violence that would shock the world.

MWANGA II, the last king of an independent Buganda

CHAPTER 2

Iron Fists

AMIN WINS A PLACE in the King's African Rifles.

AT THE MILITARY BASE IN JINJA, AMIN rarely went to school. Instead, he sold sweet *mandazi* pastries on the street to make money. He barely learned to read or write, and he picked up only broken English in the barracks.

But he did acquire one skill that would serve him well in the future: He learned to fight. As a teenager, Amin shot up to 6'4" tall and weighed over 200 pounds.

He earned a reputation as a bully, using his size to beat up other boys around the base.

Before long, the towering young man attracted the attention of British officers in Jinja. Amin did his best to impress the men in charge. He smiled and answered "Yes, sir" when they spoke to him. His politeness, his size, and his brutality on the street marked him as a promising recruit for the King's African Rifles.

The officers taught the young street tough to play rugby, run track, and shoot a rifle. But Amin found his true passion when he took his street-fighting skills into the ring as an amateur boxer. Amin didn't just defeat his opponents; he assaulted them. He had a wild, lunging style, and he fought with a cruel intensity. He battered other young boxers with a determination that worried adults who watched him. "I was seriously concerned," recalled a doctor who worked with the boxers. "He was hitting with all his force. Too much. I feared he would kill someone."

When Amin was 18, he was invited to join the King's African Rifles. He started as a cook and was promoted to corporal two years later. Soon after, he got his first taste of real warfare.

Amin's unit was sent to northeastern Uganda, along the border with Kenya, another British colony. Rival ethnic groups in the region had been stealing each

SOLDIERS OF THE KING'S AFRICAN RIFLES march on rioting Africans in the 1950s. Amin was accused of torture and murder while conducting similar peacekeeping missions in Kenya.

other's cattle for decades. A new round of fighting had broken out, and Amin's orders were to disarm the combatants and stop the violence.

The methods he used proved to be ruthlessly effective. Amin led his soldiers into village after village along the border and demanded that the men surrender their spears and their buffalo-hide shields. If the villagers refused, Amin ordered them to line up before his soldiers. Wielding a machete, he threatened to cut off the genitals of one man at a time until they revealed where their weapons were hidden.

When Amin returned from his expedition, rumors of his cruelty followed him back to Jinja. But instead of disciplining Amin, the British officers praised him for his effectiveness and marked him for promotion.

In the ring and on the battlefield, the street fighter had found a place where his strong-arm tactics were rewarded.

CHAPTER 3

Mau Mau

The young corporal commits more atrocities and GETS A PROMOTION.

AMIN'S NEXT TEST CAME IN 1952. THE KAR was ordered back to Kenya. There, the Kikuyu people had launched a rebellion against the British.

For several decades, British settlers had been forcing the Kikuyu off their land. Some 12,000 square miles of the most fertile fields in Kenya had been seized since 1900. Thousands of Kikuyu were forced to labor for British landowners or migrate to the cities in the hope of finding work.

In 1952, a group of Kikuyu decided to fight back. They organized a rebel group known as the *Muingi*—or the "Mau Mau," as the British referred to them. They vowed to drive their British overlords out of Kenya. Small bands of Mau Mau fighters burned the houses of British settlers and slaughtered their cattle. The Mau Mau also threatened Kenyans who refused to join the rebellion.

In retaliation, the British ordered troops from Uganda and their other African colonies to hunt down the rebels. The soldiers swept through rain forests and mountain highlands, searching for Mau Mau hideouts. They put Kenya's capital city of Nairobi under military control and jailed 15,000 Kikuyu.

In the mountains and forests of Kenya, soldiers of the King's African Rifles overwhelmed bands of poorly equipped Kikuyu rebels. According to some reports, Amin's E Company and other units mutilated the bodies of rebel leaders and put them on display as a warning to other Kenyans.

SUSPECTED MAU MAU REBELS are led away for
questioning after being captured in a raid in 1952.

By the end of 1955, the British and their African
troops had crushed the uprising. An estimated 50,000
Africans were dead and 70,000 more had been placed in
prison camps.

The suppression of the Mau Mau uprising would
be remembered as one of the darkest episodes in the
history of British colonialism.

For his part in it, Idi Amin was promoted to *effendi*, or warrant officer.

At the time, effendi was the highest rank an African could achieve in the British colonial army. The Mau Mau uprising, however, had set in motion a massive transformation that would open new doors for African officers and politicians all across the continent.

Despite their defeat, the Mau Mau rebels had struck a fatal blow against the British Empire in Africa. They inspired protest movements throughout the continent. It cost the British army a small fortune to suppress each rebellion. And the brutal violence that resulted damaged Britain's reputation throughout the world.

In the late 1950s, the British made plans to end seven decades of colonial rule in Africa. One by one, the British colonies in Africa would gain their independence. The liberated countries would need African officers to command their armies, so the British began to train promising recruits.

In Uganda, Amin stood out as a prime candidate. He loved the military, with its tight discipline and rigorous training. He kept his boots polished to a bright shine and his uniform crisply pressed. He may have been uneducated, but so were most of the KAR's rank-and-file troops. Uganda's colonial battalion was filled with young men who, like Amin, came from the poor communities of the north. The fact that Amin shared their roots made it easy for him to command their loyalty.

Amin had also become something of a national celebrity. He had won the army's boxing title in 1951. Soon after, he became Uganda's light heavyweight champion and defended his title in fight after fight.

Rumors about Amin's cruelty on the battlefield still circulated around the military barracks in Uganda. But the British were willing to ignore the accusations— until evidence of a new killing spree arose, just as Uganda was about to become an independent nation.

CHAPTER 4

Trouble for the Future

On the eve of independence,
another rampage nearly
DIMS THE RISING STAR
of the Ugandan army.

IN THE DRY SEASON AT THE START OF 1962,
Amin returned to the Kenyan border on a new mission.
He wore the stripes of a lieutenant now, as one of only
two native-born officers in the Uganda Rifles.

Amin had been to the border region once before,
on his first official mission, and troubling rumors had

followed him back. This time, his cruelty in the field produced more than just rumors.

Once again, Amin's task was to disarm cattle rustlers. Word quickly spread that troops from Uganda were shooting villagers and leaving their bodies to be eaten by roving packs of hyenas. Some villagers had been threatened with dismemberment if they failed to hand over their weapons. In one village, eight men were mutilated before the ninth gave up the information.

Shortly after Amin began his mission, Sir Walter Coutts, the British governor of Uganda, got a call from the deputy governor of Kenya. Some "pretty fearful" things were going on in the Turkana district of Kenya, the deputy governor reported. In one Turkana village, a dozen men had been beaten to death. Autopsies determined that their chests had been crushed. The victims had been either beaten with heavy hammers or stomped to death. In another village, several men had been tortured and executed, and their families were forced to bury the bodies.

According to reports from the field, the man responsible for the abuses was Lieutenant Idi Amin.

The deputy governor of Kenya demanded that Amin be arrested, stripped of his rank, and tried as a criminal. Coutts agreed that Amin should be disciplined. But the British governor didn't have much time left in office. The people of Uganda had just elected their own prime minister, a former schoolteacher named Milton Obote. He was scheduled to take over in October, when Uganda was to gain its independence from Britain.

Coutts went to Obote and urged him to take action against Amin. Obote decided he couldn't bring criminal charges against one of the two highest ranking African officers in the army. The trial might cause unrest among Amin's loyal troops, something Obote couldn't risk on the eve of independence.

Instead of having Amin arrested, Obote merely recommended that he receive a "severe reprimand."

In one of the last acts of Uganda's colonial government, a British court of inquiry cleared Idi

Amin of wrongdoing in the Turkana murders. Rather than suffering punishment for the barbaric acts he committed, Amin received another promotion.

And so, when the Republic of Uganda was born on October 9, 1962, Idi Amin attended independence ceremonies in the glittering uniform of a captain in the new Ugandan army.

Years later, a prediction from Governor Coutts still rang in Obote's ears. "I warn you," Coutts had said when he recommended Amin for a court-martial, "this officer could cause you trouble in the future."

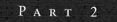

PART 2

A BLOODY POWER STRUGGLE

CHAPTER 5

A New Nation

THE REPUBLIC OF UGANDA
is formed with great hope—
and fear—for the future.

THE SOLEMN CEREMONY BEGAN WITH the slow parade of an honor guard that included the towering figure of Captain Idi Amin of the Uganda Rifles. Tens of thousands of spectators stood in hushed silence as the soldiers marched in formation through the streets of Kampala to the reviewing stand. Members of the British royal family stood next to the outgoing British governor and the incoming prime minister of Uganda. Dignitaries from around the world stood nearby to witness the historic birth of a new nation.

Amin stood at attention as the British flag was lowered. A slow drumbeat sounded as the duke of Kent, representing Her Majesty the Queen of Great Britan, stepped forward and surrendered his sword. In a symbolic act that marked the end of British rule in Uganda, the duke's sword was broken in half.

Along with thousands of his countrymen, Amin swelled with pride as the flag of the Republic of Uganda was raised for the first time. Trumpets sounded and cannons boomed a salute. The Uganda Police Band played as a choir sang the new national anthem. The archbishop of the Anglican Church of Uganda offered a prayer that God "look with mercy upon us thy people of Uganda." The leading Muslim cleric asked Allah to "Protect this nation from the shedding of blood."

And so, amid prayers for peace, the new nation was born.

THREE YOUNG UGANDANS IN KAMPALA
celebrate their country's independence. Uganda
became independent on October 9, 1962.

But even as they celebrated, most people knew it would take more than prayers to keep the peace in Uganda. The British had united 30 ethnic groups into a single nation. But in many ways, colonial rule had only aggravated hostilities among the peoples of the region.

The Bugandans in the south had grown wealthy by cooperating with the British. Their sprawling province was home to Kampala, the nation's capital. They had worked as tax collectors for the colonial government, making themselves hated in the other regions of Uganda. With help from the British, they set up large plantations to grow cotton for export. They used the profits to send their children to Christian schools to learn to read and write.

By contrast, the ethnic groups of the north remained poor. They were culturally different from the people of the south. Some worshipped as Muslims, and many spoke Sudanese or Nilotic languages rather than the Bantu languages common in the south. They resented the Bugandans for profiting from British rule.

The authors of Uganda's new constitution tried to keep the peace by creating a balance of power. Each ethnic group was represented in the national parliament. The kabaka (king) of Buganda, Mutesa II, served as the nation's president. He shared executive power with Prime Minister Obote, who came from a powerful northern ethnic group called the Langi.

From the start, Obote and Mutesa worked uneasily together. Both leaders wanted to rule Uganda without the other's interference, and they competed openly for power.

Prime Minister Obote chose Amin as his main ally in the army. This caused a conflict with Amin's boss, a Bugandan named Shabani Opolot. Opolot was a firm supporter of President Mutesa. In fact, he had married into the Bugandan king's family.

Shortly after independence, Amin and Opolot began to maneuver for control of the armed forces.

THE KABAKA OF BUGANDA, MUTESA II, became Uganda's first president. Buganda was a wealthy kingdom in the southern part of the country.

Opolot recruited well-educated young officers from his home province to bolster Buganda's role in the army. Amin detested Opolot's young, smart officers. To strengthen his own support, he recruited soldiers from the north, including his fellow Kakwas and other Sudanese speakers. He began training his recruits secretly in a forest near Jinja.

As the two military leaders maneuvered, tensions rose between Prime Minister Obote and President Mutesa. A showdown loomed, and Amin made sure he stood right in the center of the conflict.

MILTON OBOTE was elected prime minister of Uganda in 1962. Like Amin, he was from the northern part of the country. Obote had risen to power by creating an alliance of several rival Ugandan ethnic groups.

A DIVIDED COUNTRY

WHEN THE BRITISH CREATED UGANDA, THEY forced more than 30 ethnic groups, including four kingdoms, together into a single nation. Few of the groups spoke the same language, and many had long-standing conflicts.

The southern part of the country was home to the wealthier, more powerful groups, including the four kingdoms—Buganda, Bunyoro, Toro, and Ankole. The southerners spoke Bantu languages and were dominated by Buganda.

The ethnic groups of the north were poorer and culturally different from those to the south. Most spoke Nilotic and Sudanese languages, and some worshipped as Muslims. Idi Amin's Kakwa people came from the West Nile district in the north.

Under Uganda's new constitution, power was supposed to be shared among the different ethnic groups. The country's prime minister, Milton Obote, came from a northern group called the Langi. He shared power with the king of Buganda, Mutesa II, who served as Uganda's first president.

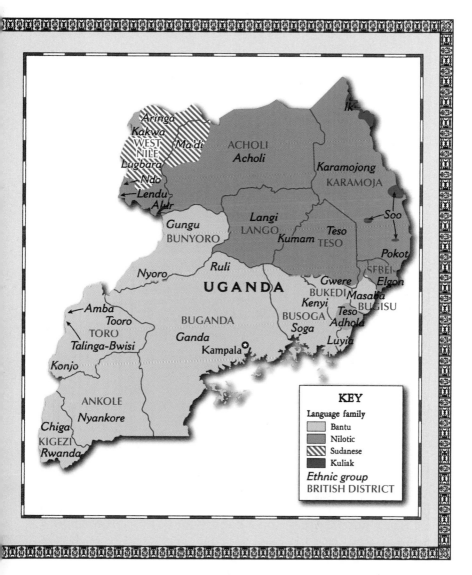

Ik

Aringa
Kakwa
WEST
NILE **Ma'di** **ACHOLI**
Lugbara *Acholi*
Ndo **Karamojong**
Lendu **KARAMOJA**
Alur

Gungu **Langi** **Soo**
BUNYORO **LANGO** **Teso**
Kumam **TESO**

Nyoro **Ruli** **Pokot**
UGANDA **SEBEI**
Gwere **Elgon**
Amba **BUKEDI** **Masaba**
Tooro **Kenyi** **Teso** **BUGISU**
TORO **BUGANDA** **BUSOGA** **Adhola**
Talinga-Bwisi *Ganda* **Soga** **Luyia**
Kampala ✚

Konjo

ANKOLE
Nyankore

Chiga
KIGEZI
Rwanda

KEY

Language family

☐ Bantu
☐ Nilotic
▨ Sudanese
■ Kuliak

Ethnic group
BRITISH DISTRICT

45

CHAPTER 6

Death of Democracy

OBOTE SEIZES CONTROL— with Idi Amin at his side.

IN 1965, THE UNEASY PEACE BETWEEN Prime Minister Obote and President Mutesa neared the breaking point. Obote had opposed Mutesa in a land dispute between the Bugandans and the people of a neighboring district. He had also promoted Amin without Opolot's consent. And in the spring, he sent Amin and his troops on a controversial mission without consulting Opolot.

Amin's mission took him back to northwestern Uganda, the land of his birth. Across the border in the Democratic Republic of the Congo, rebels were fighting a losing battle against their government. Amin was to provide weapons and sanctuary for the rebels so they could continue their fight.

Amin set up a thriving arms trade with the Congolese rebels. As the rebels retreated through Congo to the Ugandan border, they looted a fortune in gold and ivory from villages along the way. They used their loot to buy weapons from Amin.

CONGOLESE GOVERNMENT TROOPS guard rebel prisoners at gunpoint. In 1965, Obote sent Amin to give weapons to the rebels in exchange for stolen gold.

Back in Kampala, word began to leak out that Amin was keeping piles of money from the operation and splitting it with Obote. Rebels were seen delivering gold and ivory by the truckload to Amin's house. Henry Kyemba, who was Obote's private secretary at the time, noticed that Amin began carrying huge wads of cash in the overstuffed pockets of his uniform. An Israeli military adviser claimed that Amin handed him a solid gold bar worth tens of thousands of dollars and bragged that he had "five truckloads, 15 tons of this stuff." Newspapers in Great Britain started calling Obote and Amin "the gold-dust twins."

As the evidence mounted, President Mutesa's supporters in the parliament demanded an investigation. Obote took their accusations as a declaration of war. He claimed that Mutesa was plotting to get rid of him and rule Uganda as a dictator.

Then Obote proceeded to beat him to it.

In February 1966, Prime Minister Obote declared a state of emergency in Uganda. He suspended the constitution and disbanded the parliament. He ordered the arrest of five cabinet ministers who had sided with President Mutesa. Then Obote removed Mutesa from office, and on April 15, declared himself president.

In response, the Bugandans threatened to declare independence from Uganda.

To prevent the country from splintering, Obote cracked down even harder. He ordered the arrest of Mutesa's top aides.

Uganda now stood on the verge of civil war. In May, enraged crowds of Mutesa's supporters gathered in Kampala and hurled rocks at government cars. They set up barricades to block roads leading into the capital. As the tension mounted, protesters gathered at Mutesa's sprawling palace compound just outside the city and waited for a showdown.

On May 24, Colonel Idi Amin arrived outside Mutesa's compound in an open jeep armed with a six-foot-long machine gun. He ordered a battalion of soldiers to surround the compound's fortified walls.

Inside the walls, 120 well-armed Bugandan troops stood guard over the compound, which included Mutesa's palace, office buildings, a school, and several homes.

Amin ordered his soldiers to attack the compound. But for several hours, Mutesa's tiny force fought Amin's battalion to a standstill.

Finally, at 3:30 P.M., Amin halted the assault and drove his jeep to Obote's headquarters in Kampala. Amin reported that victory was certain—if Obote would permit him to use artillery against the kabaka's compound.

Permission was granted.

"[Amin] was in a jolly mood and obviously enjoying the fight," Kyemba later recalled. "He jumped into his jeep and drove off."

Amin sped back to Mutesa's compound and ordered his artillerymen to open fire. Explosive shells blasted holes in the outer walls, and Amin's soldiers stormed the palace. To their surprise, they met no resistance Mutesa had escaped and gone into hiding.

Deprived of the chance to arrest Buganda's king, Amin's troops took revenge against the Bugandan people. They arrested hundreds of Mutesa's supporters, including the army commander, Opolot. Hundreds of Bugandans were executed. Over the next few days Amin's soldiers burned homes and looted the king's luxurious palace. Drums, spears, crowns, and other treasures of the Bugandan nation were either stolen or destroyed.

At 5:30 on the day of the assault, Amin returned triumphant to Obote's lodge. He carried with him two symbolic trophies of victory: Mutesa's presidential flag and the hat that Opolot had worn as commander in chief of the Ugandan army. The hat and the job it represented now belonged to Colonel Idi Amin.

Three and a half years after Ugandans celebrated the hopeful birth of their republic, democracy in the new nation was dead.

CHAPTER 7

Setting the Stage

Is the nation's top army commander plotting to ASSASSINATE THE PRESIDENT?

TWO DECADES AFTER JOINING THE KING'S African Rifles as a cook, Idi Amin had finally risen to the top of the Ugandan army. He wore the commander's hat—and he used his new position to seize even more power for himself.

Amin continued to recruit troops from the Kakwa and Sudanese ethnic groups. Soldiers from the Langi, Acholi, and other groups still made up a large part of

AFTER 1966, Idi Ami exercised command over Uganda's army and air force. He used the position to begin plotting against the man who had promoted him—Milton Obote.

the army. But little by little, Amin was developing a force that owed its loyalty as much to him as to the country as a whole. It was, in a sense, his own private army. And he was thinking about using it against Obote.

President Obote, meanwhile, had begun to roll back the basic freedoms he had promised Ugandans. He deployed a special force of police thugs who patrolled sports arenas and city streets, hunting for any sign of dissent. Jails began to fill with political prisoners. Lists of detainees—80 names long—appeared each week in the *Uganda Gazette.*

In December 1969, a Bugandan who had eluded Obote's police nearly ended the dictator's life. President Obote was leaving a meeting in downtown Kampala when a shot rang out from behind a tree. The president fell, blood streaming from his face. A hand grenade rolled to within inches of his body—but failed to explode.

As an ambulance carried Obote to the hospital, two officers rushed to Amin's home to give him the news. When Amin saw the soldiers running toward his door, he didn't wait to hear what they wanted. He didn't even wait to put on his shoes. Uganda's top military leader ran from his house barefoot and climbed over the barbed-wire fence that surrounded his home. On bleeding feet, he ran to a side street and flagged down a car. The driver took him 30 miles north to a base camp that housed one of Amin's loyal army units.

When officials finally tracked him down, Amin said he had thought the soldiers were coming to kill him.

Amin's strange behavior that day left Ugandans wondering whether he had been involved in the assassination plot and thought he had been discovered. A group of Bugandans was eventually convicted of the crime. But Amin came under harsh criticism for his disappearance. His second-in-command, Pierino Okoya, openly accused him of desertion and called for a court-martial.

Several days later, intruders shot Okoya and his wife to death at their home.

President Obote survived the assassination attempt and several more in the months to come. But every day, he grew more suspicious of the people around him. Amin, with the power of his loyal soldiers behind him, headed the list.

Obote ordered an investigation into the deaths of Okoya and his wife and tried to fix the results to find Amin guilty. Convinced he was about to be arrested,

Amin decided to confront President Obote directly. He marched into Obote's office and drew his pistols from the holsters he wore at his hip like an Old West gunfighter. Amin handed the two six-shooters to the shocked president and declared his loyalty.

"If you don't believe me," Amin said, "shoot me."

Obote refused—and he soon lived to regret it.

CHAPTER 8

Lightning Strike

Amin seizes control of Uganda
AT GUNPOINT.

IN JANUARY 1971, PRESIDENT OBOTE prepared to fly to the Southeast Asian nation of Singapore for a meeting of world leaders. In keeping with a new custom, Idi Amin and other top officials gathered at the airport to see the president off.

Obote greeted most of his ministers warmly, but he openly ignored Amin. Henry Kyemba, who was traveling with Obote, was shocked to find Amin alone in a small room while the other officials gathered around the president.

Kyemba knew that the tension between President Obote and his top general could have dangerous consequences for Uganda. Eager to smooth things over, he approached Amin and started a conversation. Amin seemed to appreciate the courtesy, and Kyemba promised to bring him a gift from Singapore.

Then the presidential plane took off, leaving Uganda to the mercy of Idi Amin.

A week later, Obote got word that Amin was plotting to assassinate him when he returned to Uganda. The president immediately ordered his military commanders in Kampala to arrest Amin.

When Amin heard that his plot had been exposed, he didn't hesitate to act.

On the afternoon of January 24, squads of soldiers loyal to Amin took over the government radio station. Other units took tanks from the federal armory and surrounded government buildings in Kampala. Amin's troops fanned out through the capital and arrested key members of Obote's government.

THREE DAYS AFTER AMIN'S coup in January 1971,
a Sherman tank stands guard outside his home in Kampala.
Amin had seized power while President Obote was
attending a conference in Singapore.

Their orders were to shoot anyone who resisted or tried
to flee.

Within hours, Amin controlled the capital. His
soldiers began to occupy all military bases and armories
throughout the country. Many officers loyal to Obote
were arrested and imprisoned. By the next morning,
the coup was over. It had been conducted quietly and
efficiently. For Amin, it was a complete success.

For a short time, disturbing signs of violence could be seen on the streets of Kampala. A handful of bullet-riddled vehicles were abandoned throughout the city and at Entebbe Airport. Their passengers—government officials and army officers loyal to Obote—had been machine-gunned as they tried to leave the city during the night. Two priests were killed in the crossfire at Entebbe when one of Amin's tanks raked the terminal with machine-gun fire.

Many Ugandans ignored the ominous signs and hailed their new leader as a hero. After five years living under Obote's increasingly harsh regime, people were happy to see the president thrown out of office.

Amin proudly declared himself the new president of Uganda. On his first day in office, he declared an amnesty for all members of the former government—except for Obote himself. Amin's rival was to be arrested and brought back to Uganda, dead or alive.

Kyemba returned cautiously from Singapore, half expecting to be arrested. Surprisingly, Amin gave him

IDI AMIN is sworn in as Uganda's president on February 6, 1971.

a warm welcome. He asked whether Kyemba brought back the present he had promised. The bewildered aide stammered that yes, he had a radio for Amin and a bolt of cloth for his wife.

Amin grinned and laughed and thanked Kyemba for the gift. He had one for Kyemba as well. "Go home for the weekend and come back on Monday," Amin said. "Go back to your office and continue as if nothing had happened."

As Kyemba drove home from the president's lodge that afternoon, everything looked normal. The bullet-riddled cars had been removed from the streets.

Amin's soldiers had covered their tracks neatly.

IDI AMIN IN PICTURES

SERVING BRITAIN

Queen Elizabeth II inspects the King's African Rifles, a colonial army that fought for British interests in East Africa. Idi Amin joined the King's African Rifles in 1946.

MAU MAU REBELLION

In 1954, Idi Amin and the King's African Rifles were sent to Kenya to crush a group of Africans—known as the Mau Mau—who were rebelling against British control. Amin committed war crimes during this bloody campaign.

A NEW IMAGE

On October 9, 1962, Ugandans celebrated their independence from Great Britain. The shirts worn by the people to the right show Uganda's first president, Edward Mutesa.

POWER HUNGRY

Milton Obote was elected prime minister of independent Uganda. He was supposed to share power with President Mutesa. But in 1966, Obote seized power with the help of Amin and declared himself president.

BEHIND THE WHEEL

Idi Amin waves to a cheering crowd three days after overthrowing Milton Obote in 1971. Ugandans hoped Amin would be an improvement over Obote's bloody dictatorship.

OUT OF CONTROL

A former boxing champion, Amin was a national hero when he took power. Here, he prepares to fight a exhibition match against Uganda's national boxing coach. Amin shocked the crowd by brutally pummeling his opponent until the man collapsed.

ROBBED

In 1972, Amin expelled all Ugandan-Asians from the country and confiscated their property.

SHARP TURN

Idi Amin meets with Yasser Arafat, chairman of the Palestinian Liberation Organization. Amin allied with Arafat and other Muslim leaders after Amin's crimes caused Israel and Great Britain to stop giving military aid to Uganda.

RAID ON ENTEBBE

In 1976, Amin allowed pro-Palestinian terrorists with a planeload of hostages to land at Uganda's Entebbe Airport. Amin was humiliated when Israeli commandos freed the hostages in a daring midnight raid.

KILLING GROUNDS

These are skulls from a mass grave of Ugandans killed by Idi Amin's soldiers. As many as 500,000 people may have been murdered during Amin's reign.

EGOMANIAC

When Idi Amin first seized power, he promised to step aside as soon as elections were held. Later he named himself "President for Life" and loaded his uniforms with medals.

NO MERCY

Amin murdered for money, to maintain power, and for revenge. In 1977, Archbishop Janani Luwun (right) dared to speak out against the bloodshed. Amin responded by having Luwun executed.

ASHAMED OF AMIN

President Julius Nyerere of Tanzania hides his face as he shakes hands with Idi Amin in 1973. Nyerere opposed Amin's brutal regime and had denounced Amin's expulsion of Ugandan-Asians.

DEADLY DISASTER

Amin's inept rule destroyed Uganda's economy. About 50,000 Ugandans—half of them children—died in a famine that began at the end of Amin's reign.

LIBERATED!

Ugandans cheer as Tanzanian tanks roll into the city of Jinja. After eight years, Idi Amin was driven from power by an invasion backed by President Nyerere of Tanzania.

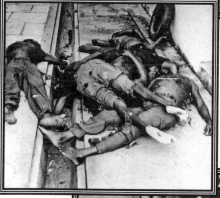

FINAL CRIMES

Tanzanian soldiers discovered this crime scene in Amin's State Research Bureau. These men had been killed so they couldn't testify to the abuses committed by Amin's secret police.

SHATTERING LEGACY

This photo of Amin was found in his ransacked office. It would take decades for Uganda to recover from Amin's murderous and corrupt regime.

PART 3

REIGN OF TERROR

CHAPTER 9

Victory Tour

AMIN CHARMS HIS PEOPLE into thinking he just might be the savior of Uganda.

IN THE WEEKS AFTER THE COUP, IDI AMIN became a celebrity, in his own country and the rest of the world.

The new president promised to bring democracy back to Uganda. He said he would hold free and fair elections soon for the parliament and the presidency. And he reached out to his old adversaries. He released 55 political prisoners who had been languishing in jail since the storming of President Mutesa's palace. Amin even set his old rival Opolot free and gave him the salary he would have earned during the five years he spent in prison. Mutesa had died in London three years earlier, but Amin had his body brought back to Buganda and arranged for an elaborate burial ceremony.

Governments around the world sent their best wishes and congratulated Amin for ousting Obote. Newspapers referred to the military takeover as a "bloodless coup." Obote had gone into exile in Tanzania and managed to keep some African governments from supporting Amin. But Uganda's two strongest allies, Great Britain and Israel, quickly recognized Amin's new government and promised large amounts of military and economic aid.

Amin seemed drunk with his sudden popularity. He traveled constantly for a month, crisscrossing the country by helicopter. Everywhere he went, people gathered to greet him. He wore a simple soldier's uniform and smiled and waved as he walked through the crowds.

IDI AMIN DRIVES TO A CEREMONY for the release of 55 political prisoners who had been jailed by former President Obote. Amin said he drove his jeep himself "just to show that I am in command."

Villagers danced and sang for the president, and Amin beamed with obvious pleasure. At some stops he joined in ceremonial dances and played the accordion. When villagers presented him with gifts, he clapped like a child opening presents at a surprise party. At one stop, local ranchers gave him an entire herd of cattle—more than 900 head—as a present.

In return, Amin showered his people with wild promises. According to Kyemba, he made his ministers follow him from village to village and ordered them around in front of the crowds. When Amin visited a place with poor health care, for example, he would introduce the minister of health and command him to build a hospital. At an isolated village Amin might point to the minister of works and communications and announce, "He will build you a road from here to there."

Amin's charm and his promises inspired hope in poor villages throughout the country. People felt as though their new leader cared about them, and they began to refer to him as "Big Daddy."

There may have been signs that "Big Daddy" had a darker side. There were the bullet-torn cars whisked away after the coup and the grim-looking soldiers with automatic weapons who guarded Amin in public.

But people chose to believe the best about their charismatic new leader—until the truth became too hard to ignore.

CHAPTER 10

Bloodbath

The so-called "bloodless coup"
gives way to a
REIGN OF TERROR.

IDI AMIN'S VICTORY TOUR PUT A FRIENDLY
face on the new Ugandan government. But while the
president charmed the public, ominous reports began
to leak out from remote army bases and high-security
jails. Prisoners escaped and whispered their tales to
friends before going into hiding. Obote supporters fled
across the border and told frightening stories to foreign
reporters.

As the evidence mounted, it began to look as though Amin's "bloodless" coup was rapidly turning into a bloodbath.

Before Amin seized power, the Ugandan army drew many of its soldiers and officers from the Acholi and Langi peoples. These men had always shown loyalty to Obote, who was a Langi. When Amin took over, some of them scattered, went into hiding, or gathered in remote areas to decide whether to oppose the coup.

Amin made the same promise to the Acholi and Langi soldiers that he had to Obote's former ministers: Return to duty and you will be treated well. The soldiers who took him up on the offer regretted it for the short time they had left.

In February and March 1971, troops loyal to Amin began rounding up Acholi and Langi soldiers all across the country. Nearly every day, trucks pulled up to the Makindye prison in Kampala. Guards led bound and beaten prisoners into the jail, prodding them along with bayonets. The military police who ran the prison named one cell "Singapore," referring to the nation Obote had been visiting when he was ousted. Another was called "Dar es Salaam," after the city in Tanzania where Obote went into exile.

While Amin was still proclaiming his devotion to democracy, Makindye became a virtual death camp. Most prisoners who were taken to the "Singapore" cell did not come out alive. The soldiers who executed them were instructed to use bayonets and machetes to avoid wasting bullets.

Joshua Wakholi, a top minister in Obote's government, witnessed some of the killings from a neighboring cell. On the morning of March 6, Wakholi and his cellmates were ordered to clean "Singapore" after 36 officers had been hacked to death there. The blood, Wakholi remembered, "was a quarter of an inch deep on the floor."

An army barracks in Kampala known as Malire served as another killing ground. On March 7, guards there locked 32 Langi and Acholi officers into a room packed with explosives. The blast could be heard for miles.

When rumors about the explosion began to spread, a spokesman for Amin announced that there was nothing to worry about. The army had merely been destroying a "damaged bomb." In the coming days, the spokesman warned, "there are still a few more damaged bombs to be destroyed."

As the spring wore on, the killing intensified. In April, more than 600 Acholi and Langi troops were slaughtered while trying to escape across the border into Sudan. In May, Amin gave his soldiers the right to shoot on sight if they suspected someone of committing a crime. He also gave military police the right to hold prisoners indefinitely without trial.

Amin made sure to hunt down anyone who had opposed him in the past. Several officers who had accused him of murdering Pierino Okoya in 1970 were imprisoned and later executed. Officials who had investigated Amin for pocketing gold from the Congolese rebels also disappeared. Thirteen of the army's 23 top officers vanished within months of the coup.

BUSINESSMEN ARE PUBLICLY BEATEN on the orders of Idi Amin. Almost immediately after taking power, Amin's henchmen began imprisoning and even executing Ugandans without trial.

Amin often charmed his victims into thinking they were welcome in the new Uganda. By the time they discovered the truth, it was too late.

Ahmed Oduka made the discovery in a particularly tragic way. Oduka had been the master of the Uganda Police Band, which was famous for its performance at Uganda's independence ceremonies in 1962. Just before the coup, Oduka had heard rumors of Amin's plan to assassinate Obote. He was the man who exposed the plot to Obote's supporters.

When Amin seized power, Oduka immediately fled to Kenya. But when he heard that many of his friends and colleagues were returning, he decided it might be safe to go back. Amin even sent an aide to plead with him. The president loved music, the aide said, and wanted the Police Band to have its bandmaster back.

Oduka gave in and flew to Kampala, where he met with Amin. The president thanked him in very friendly terms for coming home. As the bandmaster left the general's office, Amin bid him a warm good-bye.

As soon as the door closed, Amin turned to an army officer and told him to see that Oduka was "taken to Malire." The aide understood the orders perfectly. Amin then suggested to a minister in the room that he go along to watch the bandmaster's execution.

Thirty minutes later, the minister arrived at Malire. He found Oduka lying on the floor of a prison cell, his skull smashed in with a club.

CHAPTER 11

Without a Trace

THE DISAPPEARANCE
of two Americans draws the world's attention to Uganda.

WHEN THE SUMMER OF 1971 BEGAN, FEW people outside the borders of Uganda understood the extent of Idi Amin's crimes. Newspapers in Tanzania reported a few of the incidents. But most people thought the stories had been exaggerated by Obote supporters who were trying to discredit Amin.

Then the violence took the lives of two Americans, and the world began to pay attention.

In July, a young journalist from Detroit named Nick Stroh was in Kampala, trying to report on Amin's regime. He heard rumors about mass killings at Mbarara, an army barracks 170 miles from the capital. Amin's thugs had supposedly slashed the throats of more than 150 Acholi and Langi soldiers and then dumped the bodies into mass graves.

Despite warnings from Ugandan friends, Stroh decided to follow up on the story. He traveled to Mbarara with an American professor named Robert Siedle. At the barracks they tried to interview Major Juma Aiga, the Mbarara regiment's second-in-command.

Exactly what happened next never became clear. The interview ended in a heated argument. Stroh and Siedle were arrested and disappeared without a trace. Aiga was later seen driving Stroh's blue Volkswagen near the barracks.

The U.S. Embassy in Kampala demanded an investigation into the disappearances. After stalling for months, Amin finally set up an inquiry, headed by a

British judge named David Jeffreys Jones. Jones called his task "mission impossible," but agreed to preside over the case.

Meanwhile, the killings continued—and Amin continued to cover them up. After a massacre of prisoners at the Jinja army base, officers had the entire prison barracks bulldozed to bury the evidence. Amin insisted the prisoners had been shot in border fighting with Tanzanian soldiers. Several hundred more were gunned down during an escape attempt near the Tanzanian border. Amin called it a "minor incident" involving 15 detainees.

As the death toll climbed into the tens of thousands, Amin's thugs often skipped the difficult task of digging graves. Instead, they dumped victims into the Nile River, hoping that crocodiles would eat the bodies. But the crocodiles couldn't consume the bodies fast enough. Soon passing motorists could see swollen corpses drifting with the current and washing up on the riverbanks. Divers had to clear away 30 bodies

THESE SKULLS WERE FOUND in a mass grave of Ugandans murdered by Amin's soldiers. Amin's prime targets were Acholi and Langi soldiers, whom he believed were still loyal to Obote.

that had clogged the intake to the Owen Falls Dam's power plant.

In April 1972, a lieutenant from the Mbarara barracks escaped to Tanzania and revealed the details of Stroh's murder to Judge Jones. Stroh and Siedle, the lieutenant said, had been shot after their arrest. Soldiers dumped their bodies in a shallow grave. After the U.S. Embassy began to push for an investigation, Amin's soldiers dug up the bodies, burned them, and threw the remains in the Nile. Stroh's Volkswagen was set on fire and pushed down a slope into a remote mountain valley.

Judge Jones released his report in July. He found Major Aiga and the barracks commander to be responsible for the murders. As soon as the report came out, the judge left Uganda for good, fearing for his safety.

Amin, for his part, shrugged off the findings. The judge, he said, had a "prejudiced mind." Then he promoted the barracks commander to army chief of staff.

CHAPTER 12

About-Face

IN SEARCH OF CASH,
Amin turns his hatred on one of
Uganda's most reliable allies.

BY THE BEGINNING OF 1972, IT WAS CLEAR that Amin had made a mess of Uganda.

Everyone in the Ugandan government obeyed him out of fear, yet few people thought he had any idea how to run a country.

Amin often gave orders to his ministers during regular radio broadcasts to the nation. Government officials had to huddle around their radios for fear they would miss something and get blamed for it later.

English was the language for all official business in Uganda, but Amin struggled to speak it well. His ministers often had to guess what their orders were from long, rambling speeches. At one typical meeting Amin claimed he had seven important directives to announce. Uganda's top government officials dutifully took notes while they listened to a bizarre list of vague orders. "It is your duty to not be weak," Amin declared. "You must plan for meetings in advance. . . . You must love your leader; this is a duty of ministers. . . . You must teach people to love their leader. . . . Tell your women they must pull their socks up; the duty of the woman is the house."

While Amin doled out useless advice to his ministers, Uganda slid toward bankruptcy. Amin had no clear economic plan for the country. He promised big projects without considering how the nation would pay for them. He spent much of the government's annual budget on the military, showering large payments on officers and soldiers in order to ensure their loyalty.

Desperate for cash and military aid, Amin turned to Uganda's longtime allies, Britain and Israel. Both countries refused to give him anything substantial. Reports on the activities of Amin's death squads had become hard to ignore. And Amin made no secret of the fact that he planned to use the military aid to attack Tanzania, where Obote had taken refuge. Few foreign rulers wanted to support a war that could destabilize all of central Africa.

But one leader was willing.

Rejected by Britain and Israel, Amin turned to one of Israel's bitterest enemies for support. In February 1972, he flew to Libya, a largely Muslim country ruled by the dictator Colonel Muammar Gaddafi. The Libyan ruler offered millions of dollars in aid. In exchange, Amin promised to oppose Israel and help spread Islam throughout the world.

Amin went home and wrenched his country in a radically new direction. Muslims made up just five percent of Uganda's population, so Amin began paying

AMIN MEETS WITH MUAMMAR GADDAFI OF LIBYA
(far right) and other Muslim leaders. Amin was seeking new allies
after the British declared him to be "a tyrant, vindictive, ruthless,
moody, and stubborn as a child, often quite unamenable to reason,
pathologically suspicious, a liar and hypocrite."

people to convert to Islam. He also ordered all Israelis
out of Uganda and threatened to arrest any who stayed.

In radio broadcasts and public speeches, Amin made
wild attacks against Israel. The Israelis, he said, were
poisoning the Nile River in Uganda to kill Muslims

downriver in Sudan and Egypt. He boasted that he was training paratroopers for an invasion of Israel. In a telegram to the head of the United Nations, he praised the German dictator Adolf Hitler for killing six million Jews during World War II.

By April, the 500 Israelis living and working in Uganda had gone home. With them went valuable expertise in military affairs, health care, and other fields.

Despite Gaddafi's money, Uganda was left poorer than before. And Amin was not finished yet.

CHAPTER 13

Exodus

AMIN FORCES 50,000 ASIANS OUT OF UGANDA— and makes them leave their property behind.

A FEW MONTHS AFTER TURNING ON the Israelis, Amin found another group to blame for Uganda's troubles. He declared an "economic war" on Uganda's Asian minority.

In the 1890s, the British had brought thousands of laborers from India and Pakistan to build railroads in Uganda. The Asian laborers were treated little better than slaves. But many of them settled in Africa, and their descendants did well for themselves. They owned most of Uganda's factories and sugar plantations. They ran many of the retail stores in urban areas. At a time when few Ugandans owned cars, it wasn't unusual to see Ugandan-Asian families driving through the countryside on a Sunday afternoon.

On August 5, 1972, Amin announced that he wanted to put the economy in the hands of "black Ugandans." God, he said, had told him in a dream to expel all Asians and confiscate their homes and businesses. Some 50,000 Ugandan-Asians now had exactly 90 days to leave the country. "If they still remain," Amin's foreign minister announced, "they will soon see what happens to them."

Yasmin Alibhai-Brown, a Ugandan-born Asian who was forced to move to England, recalled Amin's words: "I will make you feel as if you are sitting on fire. Your main interest has been to exploit the economy for years and now I say to you all—Go!"

"That famous laugh gurgled up darkly and his big face beamed," Alibhai-Brown added.

People whose families had been in Uganda for generations had to pack their belongings and leave. Refugee families were allowed to take the equivalent of about 100 U.S. dollars and whatever luggage they could carry. Everything else had to be left behind; land, cars, businesses, even bank accounts had to be abandoned.

In the weeks before the November 8 deadline, Asian families streamed into Entebbe Airport. Soldiers stood guard along the way, hurling insults at parents and their children. Once the refugees reached the terminal, they were forced to pile their luggage on the floor. Soldiers searched the suitcases for valuables, ripping out linings and leaving clothes in a heap. They pocketed jewelry, personal items, and anything else worth stealing.

As Uganda's Asian community was forced into exile, Amin doled out their abandoned property to his allies in the army and the government. He would stride

UGANDAN-ASIANS ARRIVE IN LONDON after Idi Amin
expelled them. By accusing Ugandan-Asians of excluding black
Ugandans from business, Amin hoped to avoid blame for the
damage he had done to the country's economy.

purposefully through the commercial districts of Kampala
with an aide by his side. As he walked past shuttered
stores and office buildings, hotels and pharmacies, he
called out the names of army officers and ministers. The
aide furiously jotted down the names and matched them
with the properties.

The results for Uganda were disastrous. Most of the new owners had no experience running a business. When factory machines broke down, no one knew how to fix them. Store owners had no clue how to set prices. Many of them simply handed out their inventory to friends and family members and closed up shop.

Amin's "economic war" had uprooted 50,000 Ugandans and victimized the very people it was supposed to help.

C H A P T E R   1 4

Invasion

Obote tries to get rid of Amin— and THE UGANDAN PEOPLE SUFFER AGAIN.

IN THE FALL OF 1972, FORMER PRESIDENT Obote gave Amin an excuse to inflict another round of suffering on the people of Uganda.

On September 16, a small army of Ugandan exiles organized by Obote gathered across the border in Tanzania. The men packed up a meager supply of machine guns and hand grenades and loaded themselves into 27 trucks. In the early hours of the next day, they crossed into Uganda and launched a rebellion to overthrow Idi Amin.

It took fewer than two days for Amin's troops to rout the invaders. Hundreds of rebels were killed, and hundreds more were sent fleeing back to Tanzania. The battle was so one-sided that Amin brought his five-year-old son, Moses, out to watch the fighting.

After the rebels had been crushed, Amin used their invasion to justify a new wave of violence. He claimed that conspirators inside Uganda had helped plan the attack. Then he unleashed squads of assassins to punish anyone suspected of opposing his regime.

This time, Amin made little attempt to cover up the killings. Just after the invasion, he was hosting a group of African diplomats at a cocktail party in Kampala. His guests were shocked to see one of the rebel officers led in bound and stripped to the waist. Amin made a show of interrogating the prisoner in front of the diplomats. The officer was then hustled out and was executed several days later.

AMIN FAKES A FRIENDLY CHAT with deposed President Obote's cousin (center) and secretary for research (left). Both men were captured while fighting for Obote. Amin later had them executed.

Four days after the invasion, the chief justice of Uganda's supreme court, Benedicto Kiwanuka, was seized from his office in broad daylight. At 3 P.M. on September 21, several security officers drove up to the supreme court building. They strode in and handcuffed Kiwanuka. They marched him barefoot through the building and shoved him into their car while his fellow justices watched.

He was never heard from again.

Amin announced that Kiwanuka had been detained for plotting with Obote to overthrow the Ugandan government. But later—strangely—Amin blamed the chief justice's disappearance on Obote's soldiers.

In the months and years to come, Amin's death squads began to target ordinary civilians as well as soldiers and government officials. The two organizations responsible for policing the country had harmless sounding names—the Public Safety Unit and the State Research Bureau. But they performed their duties with lethal brutality. "The thugs in these units operate anywhere, at any time, and in full public view," Kyemba

MATHIAS KIWANUKA, a defensive end for the New York Giants, is the grandson of Ugandan Chief Justice Benedicto Kiwanuka. Benedicto was tortured and killed when he stood up to Amin. "My grandfather was a very revered man who changed a lot of people's lives," Mathias Kiwanuka said.

observed. "They arrest people in offices, at public functions, and in restaurants." One officer said he had gotten so accustomed to murdering people that it was "no more problem than killing a chicken."

The security police added to their salaries by stealing property, valuables, and cash from their victims. Often they killed not for political reasons, but purely for money. The police would torture victims until they signed over their bank accounts. "If a soldier wanted something, he just took it," a businessman later recalled. "He would come right into your house and if you didn't give it to him you would be killed."

In cities across Uganda, people lived in fear of the dark sedans that prowled the streets. Ordinary citizens refused to wear new clothes in public because they didn't want to appear wealthy. Drivers made sure to yield the right of way to expensive Peugeots or Mercedes-Benzes with darkened windows. "You could die if you passed a soldier's car or blew the horn to pass him," recalled one Ugandan who lived through the terror.

Without the rule of law to hold them back, Amin's thugs ran wild over the people of Uganda. In Kampala, a disco had to close because security agents murdered so many of its customers. Men were being thrown off the roof by thugs who wanted to dance with their girlfriends. If a woman refused to dance, she could suffer the same fate. "You could die because you were a pretty girl," recalled one survivor.

As the fear spread, people who could afford the trip escaped the country. Tens of thousands of Uganda's most productive citizens began new lives overseas. Survivors were left to wonder what happened to relatives who had disappeared without a trace.

Near the end of 1972, the British writer David Martin, one of the few journalists brave enough to report on the killings in Uganda, received a letter from the wife of one of Amin's victims.

Dorothy Ocan pleaded with Martin for news of her husband, Ben, whom Martin had listed as "missing, presumed dead" in a recent article. "I cannot look at the faces of my children," she said. "I have not been strong enough to tell the oldest, Angom, our 14-year-old who is away at school. . . . Please send us any scrap of news you can get. I have reached a dead end in my inquiries. I beg you, please, to let me know however terrible the news."

But Martin heard nothing more about Ben Ocan—or thousands more like him.

CHAPTER 15

The Public Mask

Despite the RISING DEATH TOLL, the world is slow to recognize Uganda's suffering.

By 1976, AMIN'S CRIMES STILL WENT MOSTLY unnoticed outside of Uganda. Reporters were given very little access to the country. They were often detained by security police and sometimes beaten. Few journalists were willing to risk their lives to report on Uganda's death squads.

David Martin managed to publish a book exposing many of Amin's atrocities. But he gathered most of his evidence from Ugandan exiles in Tanzania. Amin had ordered police to arrest him if he set foot in Uganda.

Another British reporter tried to enter the country just after the rebel invasion of September 1972. Security officers stopped him at a roadblock and accused him of spying for Obote. The officers confiscated his tape recorder—supposedly a "secret message machine"—and his notes, which they insisted were "invasion plans."

Without reliable information about the extent of Amin's killings, much of the world saw only his bizarre, often amusing, public face. Amin bragged on film that he had four wives and had fathered 18 children. He performed traditional African dances while wearing a three-piece suit. He drove his red Maserati sports cars through small villages at breakneck speeds.

Amin liked to keep foreign leaders off balance. On one hand, he posed as an angry enemy of the old colonial powers. He once convinced a group of British businessmen to carry him into a party for African

IDI AMIN
DANCES during
a celebration in
Kampala to mark an
anniversary of his
presidency.

diplomats in a sedan chair—just as generations of
Africans had been forced to carry their British rulers on
their backs.

Yet at the same time, Amin claimed to admire the
British Empire. He arrived at international ceremonies
holding a scepter like the kings of England once did.
He often appeared in public wearing traditional
Scottish caps and kilts. Sometimes he even showed up
at the Kampala Rugby Club to play the accordion and
sing rugby songs with British patrons.

People who worked closely with Amin understood his true nature. "Face to face, he is relaxed, simple and charming," one of Amin's former ministers said of him. "He seems incapable of wrongdoing. But this is no more than a facade. He kills rationally and coolly."

In the summer of 1976, Amin finally dropped the mask he wore in public. And when he did, all the world was watching.

IDI AMIN WAVES as British businessmen carry him to a party in Kampala. Amin later accused Robert Scanlon (second from left) of espionage. Scanlon was imprisoned and beaten to death with a sledgehammer.

C H A P T E R 1 6

Raid on Entebbe

Amin sides with terrorists—
AND PAYS THE PRICE.

On June 27, 1976, an Air France jet carrying nearly 250 passengers from Tel Aviv, Israel, to Paris was hijacked by pro-Palestinian terrorists. After refueling in Libya, the hijackers flew to Uganda, where they expected a warm welcome from Idi Amin.

The terrorists claimed to represent the millions of Palestinian Arabs who had been forced off their land when the state of Israel was founded 28 years earlier. The Palestinians wanted their own nation on territory claimed by the Israelis. Some pro-Palestinian groups used terrorist tactics to make their demands known. Palestinian terrorists shelled Israeli settlements, hijacked airlines, and set off bombs in public places. In 1972, a group of Palestinians murdered 11 Israeli athletes at the Olympic Games in Munich, Germany.

When the hijacked jet landed at Entebbe Airport, the terrorists received exactly the reception they had hoped for. The jet touched down before dawn on June 28. Amin's soldiers helped unload the plane and place the passengers in an unused wing of the airport.

Amin personally took charge of the situation and helped to draft the terrorists' list of demands. They wanted 53 Palestinians released from prisons in several different countries. If their demand was not met by July 4, the terrorists promised to kill their hostages.

The lives of innocent people hung in the balance, and Amin seemed almost giddy with excitement. According to Henry Kyemba, he wanted the "glory" of humiliating the Israelis while the entire world watched.

"Well, Kyemba," Amin told his aide, "now I've got the Israelis fixed up this time."

The Israelis, however, had no intention of being intimidated by Idi Amin. On the night of July 3, hours before the terrorists' deadline, four Israeli transport planes slipped across the Red Sea. They flew just 100 feet over the waves in order to avoid the radar systems of Egypt and Saudi Arabia. An hour before midnight, they touched down at Entebbe. A squad of 100 Israeli commandos jumped out and stormed the airport terminal where the hostages were imprisoned.

The raid took Amin and his men completely by surprise. Most of his officers were drinking and dancing at an airport hotel when the Israelis landed. As soon as the officers heard gunfire, they fled. Amin himself escaped to safety and remained in hiding until the shooting stopped. Nearly 50 of his soldiers—and all of the terrorists—were killed in the gun battle with the Israelis. Three hostages died in the crossfire, but the rest were hustled into the Israeli planes and flown to safety.

A HOSTAGE FROM THE AIR FRANCE HIJACKING is embraced upon her return to Israel. The hostages were rescued from Entebbe during a daring midnight raid by Israeli commandos.

The success of the lightning raid was a triumph for the Israelis and an embarrassment for Amin. A few days later, some of his soldiers were jeered in the streets of Kampala for running away from the Israelis. The soldiers waded into the hostile crowd and beat up several people.

Amin vented his anger in a different way. He lashed out at the lone hostage left in Uganda. A 75-year-old woman named Dora Bloch had choked on a piece of meat the day before the raid and been taken to a hospital for treatment. Amin sent his security forces to seize her. Frail and unable to walk, Bloch was pulled screaming from her bed. Hospital workers and patients watched in horror as the men dragged her outside, shoved her into their car, and drove off.

A few hours later, Bloch's body was found dumped by a roadside 20 miles from Kampala. She had been shot and stabbed.

A PHOTO OF DORA BLOCH and her granddaughter from 1975. Bloch was in a hospital when Israeli commandos freed her fellow hostages from Entebbe Airport in 1976. Amin had her murdered the following day.

CHAPTER 17

Losing His Grip

Paranoid and isolated, Idi Amin is finally THRUST FROM POWER.

THE MURDER OF DORA BLOCH PROVED to be the beginning of the end for Idi Amin.

Encouraged by Amin's falling reputation, Ugandan exiles in Tanzania made a series of raids across the border. Amin responded with a new round of purges, once again targeting the Acholi and Langi soldiers he suspected of supporting Obote.

Amin became convinced that his enemies were closing

in on him, and he lashed out with a new recklessness. Janani Luwun, archbishop of the Anglican Church of Uganda, had found the courage to speak out against the latest wave of violence. Amin decided to silence him.

In February 1977, Luwun and several Anglican bishops were arrested and hauled onto a hotel balcony before government officials, reporters, and a rowdy crowd of 2,000 soldiers. For three hours in the hot sun, Amin's security officers read pages of so-called "evidence" against Luwun. They claimed, falsely, that the archbishop had conspired with Obote to overthrow the government of Uganda.

IN 1977, ARCHBISHOP JANANI LUWUN (left) met with Amin to criticize the dictator's latest round of murders, which included the entire population of Milton Obote's hometown. For speaking out, Luwun was executed for treason.

When the sham trial was over, Amin asked the soldiers standing below whether the bishops were guilty. Chants of "Kill them! Kill them!" rose up from the crowd.

Several hours later, Archbishop Luwun was executed in the offices of Amin's security police.

Church leaders around the world erupted in anger. "[Amin] is the incarnation of what the Bible calls a wicked man," said Burgess Carr, head of the All Africa Conference of Churches. "He can be entertaining you in one room, while in the room next door people are being mutilated and tortured."

At long last, Idi Amin stood exposed to the world.

The once invincible dictator of Uganda now held onto power by a quickly fraying thread. After the Entebbe incident and the murder of Archbishop Luwun, several nations cut off trade with Uganda. Weakened by international sanctions—and years of neglect by Amin's inept government—Uganda's economy collapsed. Schools, hospitals, and roads sank into ruin. Poverty and hunger spread through the once prosperous land. Starving Ugandans went without basic foods such as sugar, flour, bread, and milk.

UGANDANS STAND IN LINE for a handout of sugar in Kampala. During Amin's eight years in power, the annual production of sugar shrank from 244,000 tons to 8,000 tons. The cotton, tea, and tobacco industries also collapsed.

On October 30, 1978, Amin made a desperate attempt to divert attention from Uganda's problems. He accused the Tanzanians of starting a war with Uganda. Then he sent 3,000 soldiers storming across the border.

For a month, Amin's troops ran wild. They attacked unarmed civilians, looted stores, destroyed buildings, and slaughtered livestock. They returned to Uganda with more than 2,000 kidnapped women and children, many of whom would die in captivity.

In a last burst of bravado, Amin taunted Tanzanian President Julius Nyerere. "I challenge President Nyerere in the boxing ring to fight it out," he declared. "Muhammad Ali would be an ideal referee for the bout."

For once, no one was laughing.

Nyerere took his time preparing a response that would silence Amin for good. He waited until he had amassed a force of 45,000 troops, a large number of whom were Ugandan exiles. Then in March 1979, he sent the soldiers into Uganda to topple the tyrant Amin.

The army that had terrorized its people for eight years fell apart in the face of the invasion. Entire battalions of Ugandan soldiers escaped to the north, bombing and looting their own country's villages as they fled.

Amin took to the radio and scolded his countrymen

IN 1979, TANZANIAN PRESIDENT JULIUS NYERERE sent 45,000 troops into Uganda. They met little resistance.

for running away. "Cowardly officers and soldiers who do not stand and fight will be court-martialed and executed!" he declared in one broadcast.

In another he pleaded, "Don't run away and leave rifles behind. Die for your country!"

But Amin was not about to set an example for his soldiers. He never showed his face near a battlefield. Instead he slipped out of Kampala and drove to Jinja, the town in southeastern Uganda where he began his career as a soldier. When Tanzanian troops got word of his location, he fled to the West Nile district, the region of his birth. From there he flew to Libya, where his one-time ally, Colonel Gaddafi, made it clear that he wasn't wanted. In the end, Amin landed in Saudi Arabia and was given refuge in the city of Jeddah.

Back in Kampala, Amin's hated security police killed witnesses in an attempt to cover up their crimes. Then they fled. Many of the officers were caught and beaten to death by angry mobs as they tried to escape to the countryside.

As Tanzanian tanks rolled into Kampala, the liberating army was greeted by cheering crowds. People threw flowers and danced and sang in the streets.

Their eight-year nightmare was finally over.

KAMPALANS CELEBRATE THE DOWNFALL
of Idi Amin. The new president, Yusuf Lule, called for
peace and forgiveness. "We must not indulge in the
evil acts of the regime we have just removed."

Epilogue

In the summer of 2003, 25 years after he was driven from Uganda, Idi Amin lay on his deathbed in Saudi Arabia. One of his wives appealed to the president of Uganda, Yoweri Museveni, to let Amin return so he could die in his homeland. Museveni, who fought in the army that expelled Amin in 1979, said he was welcome— as long as he was willing to "answer for his sins."

Amin never did. He died in Saudi Arabia on August 16, 2003, without paying for his crimes. During his eight years in power, Amin and his henchmen had murdered perhaps as many as 500,000 Ugandans. Soldiers, government officials, teachers, lawyers, business people, doctors, police officers, artists, photographers, journalists, engineers, politicians, and ordinary citizens alike were tortured and killed at Amin's whim. He was not punished in any way. He was never arrested, tried, imprisoned, or even fined for the suffering he caused.

Idi Amin lived a long and relatively comfortable life in exile. The Saudi government gave him an ample sum of money to live on. Amin used it to buy a house, a collection of automobiles, and time to swim, fish, and watch boxing matches on TV.

He insisted until his dying day that the accusations of mass murder were lies made up by his enemies. He told one journalist that he wanted to be remembered not as a former president, but "as a great athlete."

But despite Amin's attempts to whitewash his legacy, he will be remembered as one of history's worst tyrants. He betrayed his people's hopes for a democratic Uganda and left them in poverty and chaos.

After Amin fled Uganda, years of disastrous civil war followed. By the time order was finally restored in 1985, Uganda was one of the poorest nations in the world.

Under President Museveni's government, Uganda has enjoyed a much-improved economy and a measure of democracy. But the memory of Idi Amin's reign of terror lives on. The expulsion of Uganda's Asian merchants left the country struggling to rebuild hundreds of essential businesses. Amin's death squads left hundreds of thousands of children without parents. And the climate of fear created by Amin has taken decades to overcome.

THE RUINS OF IDI AMIN'S OFFICE, which was ransacked by Tanzanian soldiers. A photo of the disgraced tyrant lies among the debris.

TIMELINE OF TERROR

1925

c. 1925: Idi Amin is born in Uganda, a colony of Great Britain.

1946: Amin joins the King's African Rifles, a regiment of black soldiers fighting for the British Empire.

1954: Amin takes part in the brutal suppression of the Mau Mau uprising in Kenya.

1962: Great Britain grants Uganda its independence. Amin serves as the deputy commander of Uganda's army.

1966: Amin and his soldiers help Prime Minister Obote oust President Mutesa and seize control of Uganda.

1971: Amin overthrows Obote and becomes president of Uganda. He has the Ugandan army purged of soldiers from rival ethnic groups.

1972: After meeting with Colonel Gaddafi of Libya, Amin expels all Israelis and Asians living in Uganda.

1974: British journalist David Martin publishes a book that exposes Amin's crimes.

1976: Terrorists holding nearly 250 hostages fly to Uganda's Entebbe Airport, where Amin welcomes them. A week later, Israeli commandos rescue the hostages.

1977: Amin causes worldwide outrage when he executes the archbishop of Uganda's Anglican Church.

1979: President Nyerere of Tanzania sends 45,000 troops into Uganda. Amin flees to Saudi Arabia, where he spends the rest of his life in exile.

2003: Amin dies.

2003

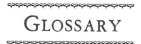

GLOSSARY

archbishop (arch-BISH-uhp) *noun* in some Christian religions, a very high ranking priest

armory (AR-mur-ee) *noun* a place where weapons are stored or soldiers are stationed

assassinate (uh-SASS-ih-nate) *verb* to murder a well-known or important person

bankruptcy (BANGK-ruhpt-see) *noun* the state of being in financial ruin and unable to pay one's debts

captivity (cap-TIV-ih-tee) *noun* the state of being imprisoned or enslaved

charismatic (kare-iz-MAT-ik) *adjective* having a powerful personal appeal

colony (KOL-uh-nee) *noun* a territory that has been settled by people from another country and is controlled by that country

constitution (kon-stuh-TOO-shuhn) *noun* the system of laws in a country that states the rights of the people and the powers of the government

controversial (kon-truh-VUR-shuhl) *adjective* giving rise or likely to give rise to public disagreement

corpse (KORPS) *noun* a dead body

coup (KOO) *noun* a sudden and illegal takeover of a government

court-martial (KORT-mar-shuhl) *noun* a criminal trial for a member of the military

democracy (duh-MAHK-ruh-see) *noun* a system of government in which the people hold the power, either directly or by voting to elect representatives

desertion (di-ZUR-shun) *noun* the crime of abandoning military duty

destabilize (dee-STAY-buh-lize) *verb* to make unstable

dismemberment (diss-MEM-bur-ment) *noun* the act of cutting off a person's limbs

exile (EG-zile) *noun* the state of being kicked out of one's homeland

kabaka (kuh-BAH-kuh) *noun* the traditional ruler of Buganda, a kingdom in southern Uganda

machete (muh-SHET-ee) *noun* a long, heavy knife with a broad blade, used as a tool and weapon

mandazi (mahn-DAZ-ee) *noun* a doughnut-like pastry popular in East Africa

Muslim (MUHZ-luhm) *noun* a person who follows the religion of Islam

mutilate (MYOO-tuh-late) *verb* to damage or injure something or someone seriously

ominous (OM-uh-nuhss) *adjective* signaling a coming evil

parliament (PAR-luh-muhnt) *noun* an assembly of elected representatives who make the laws in some countries

prejudiced (PREJ-uh-dist) *adjective* having a fixed, unreasonable, or unfair opinion about someone based on the person's race, religion, gender, nationality, or other characteristic

prime minister (PRIME MIN-ih-ster) *noun* the head of government in a country with a parliamentary system; most countries with prime ministers have both a head of government (the prime minister) and a head of state (such as a president or king)

province (PROV-uhnss) *noun* a district or region of some countries

reprimand (REP-ruh-mand) *noun* an official scolding

republic (ri-PUHB-lik) *noun* a system of government in which the people choose their leaders in free elections

rout (ROUT) *verb* to defeat completely and quickly

sanctuary (SANGK-choo-er-ee) *noun* a safe place

submission (sub-MISH-uhn) *noun* the act of surrendering to the will or authority of a superior force or another person

suppress (suh-PRESS) *verb* to hide something or stop it from happening

terrorist (TER-ur-ist) *noun* a person who uses violence or threats to achieve a political goal

tyrant (TYE-ruhnt) *noun* a person who rules in a cruel or unjust way

FIND OUT MORE

Here are some books and websites with more information about Idi Amin and his times.

BOOKS

Allen, John. Idi Amin. San Diego: Blackbirch Press, 2004. (112 pages) *Describes the events leading to Amin's rise to power, his brutal reign, how he was ousted, and what happened in Uganda after he was overthrown.*

Barter, James. Idi Amin (Heroes & Villains). San Diego: Lucent Books, 2005. (112 pages) *A well written biography of Idi Amin.*

Blauer, Ettagale, and Jason Lauré. Uganda (Enchantment of the World, Second Series). New York: Children's Press, 2009. (144 pages) *Describes the history, geography, and culture of Uganda.*

Caplan, Gerald. The Betrayal of Africa (Groundwork Guides). Toronto: Groundwood Books, 2008. (144 pages) *Explores how such Western policies as slavery, colonialism, and resource plundering—coupled with internal tyranny and corruption—have contributed to poverty, famine, and genocide in many sub-Saharan African countries (including Uganda) in the 20th and 21st centuries.*

Smith, Bonnie G. Imperialism: A History in Documents. New York: Oxford University Press, 2000. (176 pages) *First-person accounts, political documents, and dramatic photographs help tell about the expansion and decline of European empires in Africa and Asia in the 19th and 20th centuries.*

WEBSITES

http://encarta.msn.com/encyclopedia_761551632/Idi_Amin.html
MSN Encarta's online encyclopedia article about Idi Amin.

http://news.bbc.co.uk/2/hi/africa/country_profiles/1069166.stm
A BBC profile of the country of Uganda.

http://www.pbs.org/frontlineworld/rough/2007/05/uganda_the_retu.html
Uganda: The Return, *part of a PBS series of online video reports, includes interviews with and stories about Asians who were expelled from Uganda during Amin's regime.*

INDEX

Author's Note and Bibliography

As I researched the life and crimes of Idi Amin, I began to see his reign of terror as part of a long and ongoing tragedy. As enormous as his crimes were, they were not unprecedented. Long before Amin came to power, European colonial rulers used terror and exploited hostilities between ethnic groups to control their African subjects.

Amin's greatest crime may have been his failure to stop that legacy of corruption and violence from harming future generations. By adopting rather than ending the brutal practices of the colonial powers, Amin betrayed the ideals of independence and doomed his people to more years of suffering.

Hopefully, telling the story of Idi Amin and other tyrants like him will help break the cycle of violence, inter-ethnic warfare, and poverty that has brought so much misery to the people of Africa for the last half century.

Sources:

Gwyn, David. **Idi Amin: Death-Light of Africa.** Boston: Little, Brown and Company, 1977.

Kyemba, Henry. **A State of Blood: The Inside Story of Idi Amin.** New York: Ace Books, 1977.

Martin, David. **General Amin.** London: Faber and Faber, 1974.

Melady, Thomas P., and Margaret B. Melady. **Idi Amin Dada: Hitler in Africa.** Kansas City: Sheed Andrews and McMeel, 1977.

Smith, George Ivan. Ghosts of Kampala: **The Rise and Fall of Idi Amin.** London: Weidenfeld and Nicolson, 1980.

—Steve Dougherty